48 High Protein Salads for Bodybuilders:

Gain Muscle Not Fat Without Whey, Milk, or Synthetic Protein Supplements

By

Joseph Correa

Certified Sports Nutritionist

COPYRIGHT

© 2016 Correa Media Group

All rights reserved

Reproduction or translation of any part of this work beyond that permitted by section 107 or 108 of the 1976 United States Copyright Act without the permission of the copyright owner is unlawful.

This publication is designed to provide accurate and authoritative information in regard to the subject matter covered. It is sold with the understanding that neither the author nor the publisher is engaged in rendering medical advice. If medical advice or assistance is needed, consult with a doctor. This book is considered a guide and should not be used in any way detrimental to your health. Consult with a physician before starting this nutritional plan to make sure it's right for you.

ACKNOWLEDGEMENTS

The realization and success of this book could not have been possible without my family.

48 High Protein Salads for Bodybuilders:

Gain Muscle Not Fat Without Whey, Milk, or Synthetic Protein Supplements

By

Joseph Correa

Certified Sports Nutritionist

CONTENTS

Copyright

Acknowledgements

About The Author

Introduction

48 High Protein Salads for Bodybuilders

Other Great Titles by This Author

ABOUT THE AUTHOR

As a certified sports nutritionist and professional athlete, I firmly believe that proper nutrition will help you reach your goals faster and effectively. My knowledge and experience has helped me live healthier throughout the years and which I have shared with family and friends. The more you know about eating and drinking healthier, the sooner you will want to change your life and eating habits.

Being successful in controlling your weight is important as it will improve all aspects of your life.

Nutrition is a key part in the process of getting in better shape and that's what this book is all about.

INTRODUCTION

48 High Protein Salads for Bodybuilders will help you increase the amount of protein you consume per day to help increase muscle mass. These meals will help increase muscle in an organized manner by adding large healthy portions of protein to your diet. Being too busy to eat right can sometimes become a problem and that's why this book will save you time and help nourish your body to achieve the goals you want. Make sure you know what you're eating by preparing it yourself or having someone prepare it for you.

This book will help you to:

-Increase lean protein.

-Gain muscle fast naturally.

-Improve muscle recovery.

-Eat delicious food.

-Have more energy.

-Naturally accelerate Your Metabolism to build more muscle.

 -Improve your digestive system.

Joseph Correa is a certified sports nutritionist and a professional athlete.

48 HIGH PROTEIN SALADS FOR BODYBUILDERS

1. Chicken salad recipe

Ingredients:

3 skinless, boneless chicken breast halves

1 cup of chopped lettuce

5 cherry tomatoes

2 tbsp of low fat cream

1 tbsp of olive oil

1 tsp of chopped parsley

1 tbsp of sunflower oil

1 tsp of minced chili pepper

1 tbsp of lemon juice

salt to taste

Preparation:

Cut the chicken breast halves into small cubes. Mix the sunflower oil, chopped parsley, minced chili pepper and lemon juice to make a marinade sauce. Put the chicken cubes on a baking sheet, sprinkle with chili marinade and bake at 350 degrees for about 30 minutes. Remove from the oven.

Meanwhile, mix cherry tomatoes with chopped lettuce and low fat cream. Add chicken cubes and season with salt and olive oil.

Nutritional values for one cup:

Carbohydrates 12.9g

Sugar 5.1g

Protein 16.4 g

Total fat (good monounsaturated fat) 9.9g

Sodium 114.2 mg

Potassium 83.2mg

Calcium 42.4mg

Iron 0.59mg

Vitamins (vitamin A; B-6; B-12; C; D; D2; D3; K; Riboflavin; Niacin; Thiamin; K)

Calories 81

2. Red pepper salad recipe

Ingredients:

1 cup of chopped red peppers

4 eggs

1 tbsp of corn

1 small tomato

1 tbsp of olive oil

1 tsp of vinegar

salt to taste

Preparation:

Boil the eggs for about 10 minutes. Remove from the water and allow it to cool. Peel and chop into small cubes. Mix with the other ingredients and season with olive oil, vinegar and salt. Keep in the fridge for 20 minutes before serving.

Nutritional values for one cup:

Carbohydrates 13.1g

Sugar 4.8g

Protein 17.2 g

Total fat (good monounsaturated fat) 11.7g

Sodium 123.9 mg

Potassium 84mg

Calcium 42.2mg

Iron 0.35mg

Vitamins (vitamin A; B-6; B-12; C; D; D2; D3; K; Riboflavin; Niacin; Thiamin; K)

Calories 79

3. Bean salad recipe

Ingredients:

1 cup of canned beans

1 medium tomato

1.5 cup of cottage cheese

1 tsp of garlic sauce

1 tbsp of flaxseed oil

salt and pepper to taste

Preparation:

Soak the beans into water for 30 minutes. Remove and wash. Cut the tomato into small pieces and mix with other ingredients. Season with salt and pepper. Serve cold.

Nutritional values for one cup:

Carbohydrates 13.1g

Sugar 6.9g

Protein 16.7 g

Total fat (good monounsaturated fat) 9.9g

Sodium 132.4 mg

Potassium 83.9mg

Calcium 43.1mg

Iron 0.79mg

Vitamins (vitamin A; B-6; B-12; C; D; D2; D3; K; Riboflavin; Niacin; Thiamin; K)

Calories 78

4. Cottage cheese salad recipe

Ingredients:

2 cups of cottage cheese

2 tbsp of low fat cream

3 boiled egg

1 cup of chopped lettuce

1 cup of chopped cucumber

1 tsp of mint

1 tbsp of almond oil

salt to taste

Preparation:

Mash the egg and mix it with cheese and cream until smooth mixture. You can use electric mixer for this. Combine this mixture with chopped lettuce and cucumber, season with oil and salt. Sprinkle some mint on top. Serve cold.

Nutritional values for one cup:

Carbohydrates 16.4g

Sugar 9.2g

Protein 19.2 g

Total fat (good monounsaturated fat) 13.9g

Sodium 146mg

Potassium 79mg

Calcium 51.1mg

Iron 0.67mg

Vitamins (vitamin A; B-6; B-12; C; D; D2; D3; K; Riboflavin; Niacin; Thiamin; K)

Calories 95

5. Lamb cutlets with peppers salad recipe

Ingredients:

3 thin lamb cutlets

2 green peppers, chopped

1 medium tomato

½ cup of canned green beans

1 small onion

1 tbsp of vegetable oil

salt and pepper to taste

For marinade:

¼ cup of red wine vinegar

¼ cup of lemon juice

1 tsp of ground pepper

2 tbsp of vegetable oil

Preparation:

Mix the marinade ingredients in a small bowl. Soak the lamb cutlets in it and keep in the fridge for about an hour.

Remove from the fridge and fry in a grill pan, on a medium temperature, for about 15 minutes on each side. You can add some water while frying (½ cup should be enough). Remove from the grill pan and cut into small cubes.

Wash and cut tomato into thin slices. Peel and cut the onion. Mix with other ingredients, add cutlets and season with oil and salt.

Nutritional values for one cup:

Carbohydrates 15.1 g

Sugar 7.7g

Protein 17.8 g

Total fat (good monounsaturated fat) 12.8g

Sodium 143.3 mg

Potassium 95.4mg

Calcium 49.6mg

Iron 0.44mg

Vitamins (vitamin A; B-6; B-12; C; D; D2; D3; K; Riboflavin; Niacin; Thiamin; K)

Calories 99

6. Spicy green beans salad recipe

Ingredients:

½ cup of canned green beans

1 large tomato

1 cup of chopped radicchio

2 cups of canned tuna, without oil

1 tbsp of tomato sauce

1 tsp of ground chili

½ tsp of pepper

½ tsp of tabasco sauce

1 tbsp of olive oil

salt to taste

Preparation:

First you want to prepare a spicy sauce. Mix tomato sauce with ground chili, pepper and tabasco sauce until smooth mixture (you can add few drops of lemon juice, but that is optional). Wash and cut tomato, combine with other ingredients and spicy sauce. Season with olive oil and salt.

Nutritional values for one cup:

Carbohydrates 15.9g

Sugar 7.1g

Protein 19.1 g

Total fat (good monounsaturated fat) 12.1g

Sodium 167.2 mg

Potassium 73mg

Calcium 46.9mg

Iron 0.54mg

Vitamins (vitamin A; B-6; B-12; C; D; D2; D3; K; Riboflavin; Niacin; Thiamin; K)

Calories 87

7. Eggs and onions salad recipe

Ingredients:

2 medium onions

4 boiled eggs

1 grated carrot

1 cup of chopped baby spinach

1 tbsp of grated fresh ginger

1 tbsp of lemon juice

1 tbsp of olive oil

1 tsp of ground turmeric

salt to taste

Preparation:

Peel and cut the onions. Salt it and leave it to stand for 15-20 minutes. Wash and squeeze, sprinkle some lemon juice over it and leave it. Meanwhile, boil the eggs for about 10 minutes, remove from heath, peel and cut into small cubes. Combine it with baby spinach, grated carrot and ginger. Add onions and season with olive oil, salt and turmeric. Serve cold.

Nutritional values for one cup:

Carbohydrates 11.6g

Sugar 6.1g

Protein 18.2 g

Total fat (good monounsaturated fat) 8.7g

Sodium 167.9 mg

Potassium 88.1mg

Calcium 56.6mg

Iron 0.88mg

Vitamins (vitamin A; B-6; B-12; C; D; D2; D3; K; Riboflavin; Niacin; Thiamin; K)

Calories 79

8. Spicy lettuce salad recipe

Ingredients:

1 cup of chopped lettuce

2 cups of cottage cheese

½ cup of canned corn

2 chili peppers

1 tsp of ground chili

1 tbsp of lemon juice

salt to taste

Preparation:

Combine the lettuce with cottage cheese and canned corn. Cut chili peppers into very small pieces and add to the mixture. Mix the ground chili with lemon juice and pour over the mixture. Salt to taste. Serve cold.

Nutritional values for one cup:

Carbohydrates 15.8g

Sugar 8.9g

Protein 16.3 g

Total fat (good monounsaturated fat) 11.9g

Sodium 185.3mg

Potassium 99.2mg

Calcium 48.9mg

Iron 0.56mg

Vitamins (vitamin A; B-6; B-12; C; D; D2; D3; K; Riboflavin; Niacin; Thiamin; K)

Calories 89

9. Grated red cabbage salad recipe

Ingredients:

1 cup of grated red cabbage

½ cup of grated carrot

½ cup of grated beetroot

1 cup of tofu

3 tbsp of minced almonds

1 tbsp of almond extract

1 tbsp of almond oil

salt to taste

Preparation:

Mix the vegetables in a large bowl. Add tofu, minced almonds and almond extract. Season with almond oil and salt. You can add some lemon juice or vinegar, but that is optional.

Nutritional values for one cup:

Carbohydrates 13.9g

Sugar 6.1g

Protein 17.2 g

Total fat (good monounsaturated fat) 12.1g

Sodium 142.5 mg

Potassium 86.7mg

Calcium 46.9mg

Iron 0.58mg

Vitamins (vitamin A; B-6; B-12; C; D; D2; D3; K; Riboflavin; Niacin; Thiamin; K)

Calories 93

10. Bean and spinach salad recipe

Ingredients:

1 cup of canned green beans

1 cup of chopped spinach

2 cans of tuna, without oil

1 tbsp of olive oil

1 tsp of red wine vinegar

salt to taste

1 tbsp of ground turmeric

Preparation:

Combine the green beans with chopped spinach and tuna. Season with olive oil, vinegar and salt. Add some turmeric before serving.

Nutritional values for one cup:

Carbohydrates 15.9g

Sugar 7g

Protein 19.9g

Total fat (good monounsaturated fat) 13.9g

Sodium 124.7 mg

Potassium 86.9mg

Calcium 46.7mg

Iron 0.55mg

Vitamins (vitamin A; B-6; B-12; C; D; D2; D3; K; Riboflavin; Niacin; Thiamin; K)

Calories 81

11. Chicken delight salad recipe

Ingredients:

2 thin slices of skinless, boneless chicken breast

1 large onion

1 large red pepper

½ cup of canned corn

1 tbsp of low fat cream

1 tbsp of curry

1 tsp of curry sauce

1 tbsp of lemon juice

salt to taste

2 tbsp of oil for frying

Preparation:

Cut the chicken breast into medium sized cubes. Mix the oil, curry and curry sauce in a large saucepan. Add chicken cubes and fry on a low temperature for about 25 minutes. Stir well and add low fat cream and lemon juice. Remove from the heath and allow it to cool. Meanwhile, peel and cut the onion into thin slices. Combine it with chopped red pepper and canned corn. Add chicken and mix well. Salt to taste.

Nutritional values for one cup:

Carbohydrates 10.2g

Sugar 8.8g

Protein 15.1 g

Total fat (good monounsaturated fat) 9.6g

Sodium 143.4 mg

Potassium 91mg

Calcium 65.5mg

Iron 0.41mg

Vitamins (vitamin A; B-6; B-12; C; D; D2; D3; K; Riboflavin; Niacin; Thiamin; K)

Calories 87

12. Light turkey salad recipe

Ingredients:

3 thin slices of smoked turkey breast

1 cup of lettuce

1 small tomato

1 small onion

1 red pepper

1 tbsp of lemon juice

salt to taste

Preparation:

Cut the vegetables into small pieces. Combine them with turkey breast slices and season with salt and lemon juice.

Nutritional values for one cup:

Carbohydrates 13.3g

Sugar 7.6g

Protein 15.2 g

Total fat (good monounsaturated fat) 9.7g

Sodium 124mg

Potassium 89mg

Calcium 41.6mg

Iron 0.39mg

Vitamins (vitamin A; B-6; B-12; C; D; D2; D3; K; Riboflavin; Niacin; Thiamin; K)

Calories 71

13. Eggs and white cream salad recipe

Ingredients:

4 eggs

2 cups of cottage cheese

½ cup of low fat cream

1 large tomato

1 large onion

1 tbsp of minced hazelnuts

1 tbsp of lemon juice

salt to taste

Preparation:

Boil the eggs for about 10 minutes. Peel and cut into 8 equal parts. Combine with the rest of ingredients and add lemon juice and salt. Keep in the refrigerator for about 20 minutes before serving.

Nutritional values for one cup:

Carbohydrates 16.9g

Sugar 8.1g

Protein 17.9 g

Total fat (good monounsaturated fat) 9.9g

Sodium 132.8 mg

Potassium 91mg

Calcium 52.7mg

Iron 0.71mg

Vitamins (vitamin A; B-6; B-12; C; D; D2; D3; K; Riboflavin; Niacin; Thiamin; K)

Calories 92

14. Spanish omelet salad recipe

Ingredients:

For the omelet:

3 eggs

2 cups of chopped chicken breast without skin

1 red pepper

1 tsp of ground dry rosemary

oil for frying

¼ tsp of pepper

For the salad:

1 cup of chopped lettuce

½ cup of boiled broccoli

1 medium tomato

¼ cup of olives

1 tbsp of olive oil

1 tbsp of lemon juice

salt

Preparation:

First you want to make an omelet. Use a large saucepan and add some oil in it. Fry chicken on a medium temperature for about 15-20 minutes, until nice golden color, stirring constantly. Add chopped red pepper and stir well. Meanwhile, beat the eggs in a bowl and add rosemary. Mix with the meat and red pepper in a saucepan and fry for few more minutes. Remove from the heath and allow it to cool for 10 minutes.

Combine the lettuce, boiled broccoli and tomato in a large bowl. Add olives and omelet, mix well and season with olive oil and lemon juice. Salt to taste.

Nutritional values for one cup:

Carbohydrates 20.5g

Sugar 10.9g

Protein 22.4 g

Total fat (good monounsaturated fat) 15.9g

Sodium 157.9mg

Potassium 112mg

Calcium 69.9mg

Iron 0.61mg

Vitamins (vitamin A; B-6; B-12; C; D; D2; D3; K; Riboflavin; Niacin; Thiamin; K)

Calories 127

15. Arugula salad recipe

Ingredients:

1 large tomato

1 small onion

1 tbsp of ground garlic

1 cup of chopped arugula

1 cup of cottage cheese

1 tbsp of lemon juice

salt and pepper to taste

Preparation:

Wash and cut the vegetables. Combine the ingredients in a large bowl and season with lemon juice, salt and pepper.

You can add some chili, curry, turmeric or ginger, depending on your taste. This is optional.

Nutritional values for one cup:

Carbohydrates 17.1g

Sugar 11.2g

Protein 23.9 g

Total fat (good monounsaturated fat) 16.5g

Sodium 127mg

Potassium 86mg

Calcium 46.9mg

Iron 0.39mg

Vitamins (vitamin A; B-6; B-12; C; D; D2; D3; K; Riboflavin; Niacin; Thiamin; K)

Calories 90

16. Apple salad recipe

Ingredients:

1 large apple

1 cup of chopped spinach

1.5 cup of low fat cream

1 tbsp of apple juice

½ cup of canned lentil

1 tsp of apple vinegar

Preparation:

Wash and peel the apple. Cut it into thin slices. Use a large bowl to combine the apple with other ingredients. Season with apple vinegar and serve cold.

Nutritional values for one cup:

Carbohydrates 19.7g

Sugar 13.8g

Protein 21.2 g

Total fat (good monounsaturated fat) 13.9g

Sodium 120.7 mg

Potassium 80.9mg

Calcium 49.3mg

Iron 0.33mg

Vitamins (vitamin A; B-6; B-12; C; D; D2; D3; K; Riboflavin; Niacin; Thiamin; K)

Calories 79

17. Mediterranean salad recipe

Ingredients:

3 mackerel fillets, without bones

oil for frying

salt

1 tsp of ground rosemary

1 cup of cherry tomatoes

¼ cup of olives

1 tsp of ground garlic

1 tsp of ground basil

2 tbsp of lemon juice

salt to taste

Preparation:

Sprinkle the mackerel fillets with rosemary and fry in a large saucepan at 350 degrees for about 10 minutes on each side, or until nice golden color. Use a kitchen paper to soak the excess oil. Allow it to cool for about 15 minutes and cut into equal cubes.

Mix the fish with other ingredients in a large bowl. Add garlic, basil and lemon juice. Salt to taste and serve warm.

Nutritional values for one cup:

Carbohydrates 21.9g

Sugar 14.5g

Protein 24.9g

Total fat (good monounsaturated fat) 17.8g

Sodium 135.9 mg

Potassium 75.9mg

Calcium 47.9mg

Iron 0.82mg

Vitamins (vitamin A; B-6; B-12; C; D; D2; D3; K; Riboflavin; Niacin; Thiamin; K)

Calories 120

18. Tuna and olives salad recipe

Ingredients:

2 cups of canned tuna without oil

1 cup of chopped lettuce

1 small onion

½ cup of olives

¼ cup of chopped red pepper

1 tbsp of olive oil

salt

1 tbsp of lemon juice

Preparation:

Peel and cut the onion into small pieces. Combine it with canned tuna and chopped lettuce. Mix well. Add olives and chopped red pepper. Season with olive oil, salt and lemon juice. Keep in the refrigerator for about 20-30 minutes.

Nutritional values for one cup:

Carbohydrates 21.8g

Sugar 13.5g

Protein 24.1 g

Total fat (good monounsaturated fat) 11.9g

Sodium 129.5 mg

Potassium 72.8mg

Calcium 44.9mg

Iron 0.41mg

Vitamins (vitamin A; B-6; B-12; C; D; D2; D3; K; Riboflavin; Niacin; Thiamin; K)

Calories 118

19. Carrot salad recipe

Ingredients:

1 large carrot, grated

2 cups of Greek yogurt

½ cup of canned lentils

1 cup of chopped lettuce

1 tbsp of olive oil

1 tsp of apple vinegar

salt to taste

Preparation:

Mix the carrot, Greek yogurt and lentils in a bowl. Keep this mixture in the refrigerator for at least one hour. Remove from the fridge and add chopped lettuce, olive oil and apple vinegar. Mix well and serve. Salt to taste.

Nutritional values for one cup:

Carbohydrates 19.4g

Sugar 17.8g

Protein 22.1 g

Total fat (good monounsaturated fat) 18.9g

Sodium 131.9 mg

Potassium 89.6mg

Calcium 44.8mg

Iron 0.41mg

Vitamins (vitamin A; B-6; B-12; C; D; D2; D3; K; Riboflavin; Niacin; Thiamin; K)

Calories 82

20. Chicken with walnuts salad recipe

Ingredients:

3 thick slices of chicken breast, without skin and bones

1 cup of baby spinach

1 small tomato

1 cup of minced walnuts

1 tbsp of almond oil

salt to taste

Preparation:

For this salad you want to cook the chicken meat. Use a large pot and cook the chicken breast for at least 30 minutes on 350 degrees. You might want to try it before serving it. Use a fork and check if the meat is soft enough.

Remove from the pot and cut into medium sized cubes. Wash and cut the vegetables, add walnuts, chicken breast and mix well. Season with almond oil, salt and minced walnuts.

Nutritional values for one cup:

Carbohydrates 25g

Sugar 11.4g

Protein 28.9 g

Total fat (good monounsaturated fat) 19.9g

Sodium 136.5 mg

Potassium 93.8mg

Calcium 51.9mg

Iron 0.39mg

Vitamins (vitamin A; B-6; B-12; C; D; D2; D3; K; Riboflavin; Niacin; Thiamin; K)

Calories 159

21. Almond and eggs salad recipe

Ingredients:

4 eggs, boiled

½ cup of grated almonds

1 large cucumber, cut into small cubes

1 cup of cherry tomatoes

1 cup of Greek yogurt

1 tbsp of lemon juice

1 tbsp of flaxseed oil

salt to taste

Preparation:

Mash the eggs in a large bowl, with a fork. Pour the Greek yogurt and mix well. Add cucumber and cherry tomatoes and leave in the fridge for at least 30 minutes. Remove from the fridge, add grated almonds and season with lemon juice, flaxseed oil and salt.

Nutritional values for one cup:

Carbohydrates 17.7g

Sugar 10.3g

Protein 26.8g

Total fat (good monounsaturated fat) 15.2g

Sodium 156.9mg

Potassium 92.8mg

Calcium 55.7mg

Iron 0.79mg

Vitamins (vitamin A; B-6; B-12; C; D; D2; D3; K; Riboflavin; Niacin; Thiamin; K)

Calories 135

22. Lemon salad recipe

Ingredients:

1 cup of chopped lettuce

1 cup of cottage cheese

¼ cup of lemon juice

1 tsp of ground garlic

salt to taste

Preparation:

Combine the ingredients in a large bowl. Keep in the fridge for at least 30 minutes. You can add some pepper, but that is optional.

Nutritional values for one cup:

Carbohydrates 8.2g

Sugar 5.9g

Protein 10.1 g

Total fat (good monounsaturated fat) 7.6g

Sodium 131mg

Potassium 85mg

Calcium 45mg

Iron 0.34mg

Vitamins (vitamin A; B-6; B-12; C; D; D2; D3; K; Riboflavin; Niacin; Thiamin; K)

Calories 50

23. Baby spinach salad recipe

Ingredients:

1 cup of fresh baby spinach

1 cup of ground walnuts

¼ cup of sweet corn, canned

¼ cup of cooked beans

1 tsp of sunflower oil

salt to taste

Preparation:

Combine the ingredients in a large bowl. Mix well and keep in the fridge for about 30 minutes. Serve cold.

Nutritional values for one cup:

Carbohydrates 23g

Sugar 14.9g

Protein 26.1 g

Total fat (good monounsaturated fat) 11.6g

Sodium 167.9 mg

Potassium 92.8mg

Calcium 47.9mg

Iron 0.57mg

Vitamins (vitamin A; B-6; B-12; C; D; D2; D3; K; Riboflavin; Niacin; Thiamin; K)

Calories 111

24. Mixed vegetable salad recipe

Ingredients:

1 medium tomato

1 medium onion

1 cup of chopped lettuce

1 cup of chopped spinach

½ cup of chopped rucola

1 small red pepper

½ cup of grated cabbage

1 cup of cottage cheese

2 tbsp of sunflower oil

1 tbsp of apple vinegar

salt to taste

Preparation:

This recipe is very easy to prepare and it takes about 10 minutes. All you want to do is combine the vegetables in a large bowl and mix well. Season with oil and vinegar. Salt to taste.

Nutritional values for one cup:

Carbohydrates 11.2g

Sugar 8.7g

Protein 10.8 g

Total fat (good monounsaturated fat) 6.8g

Sodium 156.3 mg

Potassium 91mg

Calcium 65.5mg

Iron 0.71mg

Vitamins (vitamin A; B-6; B-12; C; D; D2; D3; K; Riboflavin; Niacin; Thiamin; K)

Calories 50

25. Mint and tuna salad recipe

Ingredients:

2 cups of canned tuna

2 medium tomatos

1 small onion

1 tbsp of dried mint

1 tbsp of olive oil

1 tbsp of lemon juice

salt to taste

Preparation:

Peel and cut the onion and tomato into thin slices. Mix with tuna and dried mint. Add olive oil, lemon juice and salt. Keep in the refrigerator for about 20-30 minutes.

Nutritional values for one cup:

Carbohydrates 17.5g

Sugar 10.1g

Protein 27.4 g

Total fat (good monounsaturated fat) 15.8g

Sodium 126.1 mg

Potassium 89mg

Calcium 44.1mg

Iron 0.39mg

Vitamins (vitamin A; B-6; B-12; C; D; D2; D3; K; Riboflavin; Niacin; Thiamin; K)

Calories 99

26. Quinoa salad recipe

Ingredients:

1/3 cup of quinoa

1 cup of chopped radish

½ cup of grated cabbage

½ cup of feta cheese

olive oil

salt to taste

Preparation:

First you want to cook the quinoa. To cook one cup of quinoa, you need two cups of water. It takes about 20 minutes, on a low temperature to cook quinoa. Remove from the heath and drain. Allow it to cool for a while.

Mix the quinoa with chopped radish and grated cabbage. Add feta cheese, olive oil and little salt.

Nutritional values for one cup:

Carbohydrates 14.5g

Sugar 10.9g

Protein 13.2 g

Total fat (good monounsaturated fat) 11.6g

Sodium 131.8 mg

Potassium 89mg

Calcium 49.4mg

Iron 0.57mg

Vitamins (vitamin A; B-6; B-12; C; D; D2; D3; K; Riboflavin; Niacin; Thiamin; K)

Calories 69

27. Sweet potato and cheese salad recipe

Ingredients:

1 medium sweet potato

1 large onion

1 cup of cottage cheese

1 tbsp of almond oil

salt

1 tbsp of chopped parsley

Preparation:

Peel and cut potato into thin slices. Add into boiling water and cook until tender. Remove from the heath, drain and allow it to cool.

Peel and cut the onion into small pieces. Salt it and let it stand for 10-15 minutes. Wash and mix with cottage cheese and potato slices. Season with almond oil, salt and chopped parsley.

Nutritional values for one cup:

Carbohydrates 18.1g

Sugar 13.3g

Protein 21g

Total fat (good monounsaturated fat) 14.9g

Sodium 139.7 mg

Potassium 84.3mg

Calcium 49.1mg

Iron 0.41mg

Vitamins (vitamin A; B-6; B-12; C; D; D2; D3; K; Riboflavin; Niacin; Thiamin; K)

Calories 103

28. Grilled broccoli salad recipe

Ingredients:

1 cup of fresh broccoli

oil for frying

1 tsp of green pepper sauce

1 cup of Greek yogurt

1 tsp of garlic extract

1 tbsp of ground basil

salt to taste

Preparation:

For this recipe you will need a grill pan. Sprinkle some oil and fry the broccoli for about 20 minutes. Stir well. You want to get a nice golden brown color of your broccoli. After about 20 minutes, add 1 tbsp of green pepper sauce, mix well and remove from the heath.

Combine the grilled broccoli with other ingredients and add a little salt. Keep in the fridge for at least 30 minutes before serving.

Nutritional values for one cup:

Carbohydrates 10.1g

Sugar 6.8g

Protein 12.1 g

Total fat (good monounsaturated fat) 8.5g

Sodium 124.1 mg

Potassium 85.2mg

Calcium 45.6mg

Iron 0.35mg

Vitamins (vitamin A; B-6; B-12; C; D; D2; D3; K; Riboflavin; Niacin; Thiamin; K)

Calories 50

29. Cottage cheese with lime dressing salad recipe

Ingredients:

2 cups of cottage cheese

1 large cucumber

½ cup of ground walnuts

¼ cup of lime juice

¼ cup of low fat cream

1 tsp of lime extract

1 tbsp of olive oil

¼ tsp of pepper

Preparation:

First you want to make a lime dressing. Mix the lime juice with low fat cream, lime extract and olive oil. Add some pepper (this part depends on your taste). Mix well and leave in the fridge for about 30 minutes. Peel and cut the cucumber into small cubes and combine with ground walnuts and cottage cheese. Pour the dressing over your salad and serve cold.

Nutritional values for one cup:

Carbohydrates 29g

Sugar 17.5g

Protein 32.1 g

Total fat (good monounsaturated fat) 21.3g

Sodium 145.4 mg

Potassium 87.3mg

Calcium 43.9mg

Iron 0.42mg

Vitamins (vitamin A; B-6; B-12; C; D; D2; D3; K; Riboflavin; Niacin; Thiamin; K)

Calories 131

30. Lentil salad recipe

Ingredients:

1 cup of canned lentil

1 small eggplant

¼ cup of low fat cream

¼ cup of lemon juice

2 tbsp of olive oil

1 tbsp of chopped parsley

1 large tomato

1 small onion

Preparation:

Peel and wash the eggplant. Cut into thin slices and combine with a low fat cream, lemon juice and olive oil. Use an electric mixer, or a blender to get a smooth mousse. Allow it to cool in the refrigerator for about 30 minutes. Meanwhile cut the vegetables into thin slices. Mix with lentil and eggplant mousse. Sprinkle with some parsley and serve.

Nutritional values for one cup:

Carbohydrates 15.2g

Sugar 9.9g

Protein 15.2 g

Total fat (good monounsaturated fat) 10.6g

Sodium 133.8 mg

Potassium 91mg

Calcium 49.1mg

Iron 0.52mg

Vitamins (vitamin A; B-6; B-12; C; D; D2; D3; K; Riboflavin; Niacin; Thiamin; K)

Calories 77

31. Seitan and curry salad recipe

Ingredients:

1 cup of chopped white seitan

1 cup of chopped lettuce

2 green peppers

1 tbsp of curry sauce

1 tsp of ground curry

1 tbsp of olive oil

salt

Preparation:

This is another quick protein salad recipe. Combine the lettuce with white seitan and chopped peppers. Add curry sauce, ground curry, olive oil, salt and mix well. Leave in the fridge for about an hour before serving.

Nutritional values for one cup:

Carbohydrates 12.2g

Sugar 5.9g

Protein 15.1 g

Total fat (good monounsaturated fat) 10.6g

Sodium 141.8 mg

Potassium 89mg

Calcium 44.5mg

Iron 0.51mg

Vitamins (vitamin A; B-6; B-12; C; D; D2; D3; K; Riboflavin; Niacin; Thiamin; K)

Calories 60

32. Mushroom salad recipe

Ingredients:

½ cup of brown rice

2 cups of fresh bottom mushrooms

1 tbsp of oil

1 large tomato

¼ cup of fresh parsley

¼ cup of lime juice

salt

pepper

Preparation:

First you need to cook the rice. Wash and rinse it and put in a saucepan with 1 cup of water. Stir well and bring to the boiling point. Cover the pan with a lid and cook for about 15 minutes on a low temperature. Remove from the heath and allow it to cool.

Now you want to prepare the bottom mushrooms. Wash and cut into a similar size pieces. Heat a frying pan on a low temperature and add the oil. Add mushrooms and stir well. Fry on a low temperature until all the mushrooms soften, or until all the water evaporates. Remove from the frying pan. Add salt and mix with rice.

Cut tomato into small cubes and combine all the ingredients with rice and mushrooms. Season with salt, pepper and lime juice. Serve warm.

Nutritional values for one cup:

Carbohydrates 18.6g

Sugar 11.3g

Protein 21.9g

Total fat (good monounsaturated fat) 14.2g

Sodium 153.3 mg

Potassium 89.8mg

Calcium 49.9mg

Iron 0.42mg

Vitamins (vitamin A; B-6; B-12; C; D; D2; D3; K; Riboflavin; Niacin; Thiamin; K)

Calories 79

33. Cucumber and yogurt salad recipe

Ingredients:

1 large cucumber

1 tsp of ground garlic

1 cup of low fat yogurt

1 tbsp of cottage cheese

Preparation:

Peel and cut the cucumber into thin slices. Mix with yogurt, cheese and garlic. Leave in the refrigerator for at least 30 minutes before serving. You can add some salt, but this is optional.

Nutritional values for one cup:

Carbohydrates 10.2g

Sugar 7.9g

Protein 11.2 g

Total fat (good monounsaturated fat) 8.6g

Sodium 120.9 mg

Potassium 81mg

Calcium 44.5mg

Iron 0.51mg

Vitamins (vitamin A; B-6; B-12; C; D; D2; D3; K; Riboflavin; Niacin; Thiamin; K)

Calories 52

34. Spring salad

Ingredients:

1 cup of chopped baby spinach

½ cup of grated cabbage

¼ cup of canned corn

1 cup of low fat yogurt

1 tbsp of lime juice

Preparation:

Combine the low fat yogurt with lime juice, mix well and leave in the refrigerator for 30 minutes.

Use a large bowl to mix baby spinach, grated cabbage and corn with lime dressing. Serve cold.

Nutritional values for one cup:

Carbohydrates 16.2g

Sugar 9.4g

Protein 19.1 g

Total fat (good monounsaturated fat) 13.9g

Sodium 144.5 mg

Potassium 86mg

Calcium 45.9mg

Iron 0.36mg

Vitamins (vitamin A; B-6; B-12; C; D; D2; D3; K; Riboflavin; Niacin; Thiamin; K)

Calories 79

35. Greek yogurt salad recipe

Ingredients:

3 tbsp of Greek yogurt

1 tbsp of Parmesan cheese

1 tsp of mustard

1 tsp of garlic

1 cup of canned green beans

1 cup of chopped lettuce

1 tbsp of olive oil

salt

Preparation:

Use an electric mixer for few minutes to mix Greek yogurt with Parmesan cheese, garlic and mustard. You want a smooth mixture. Allow it to cool in the refrigerator for about 30 minutes. Meanwhile, combine green beans with chopped lettuce and olive oil. Mix with Greek yogurt dressing and add some salt. Serve cold.

Nutritional values for one cup:

Carbohydrates 11.7g

Sugar 8.9g

Protein 10.2 g

Total fat (good monounsaturated fat) 11.6g

Sodium 133.2 mg

Potassium 84mg

Calcium 42.6mg

Iron 0.32mg

Vitamins (vitamin A; B-6; B-12; C; D; D2; D3; K; Riboflavin; Niacin; Thiamin; K)

Calories 55

36. Chickpea salad recipe

Ingredients:

1 cup of tinned, drained chickpeas

1 small tomato

1 small peeled onion

1 chili pepper, freshly ground

1 tbsp of extra virgin olive oil

1/4 tsp of sea salt

1 tsp of mustard

Preparation:

Finely slice the onion and tomato and mix them with ground chili pepper and chickpeas. Put the vegetables into a large bowl and dress with extra virgin olive oil, sea salt and mustard.

Nutritional values for one cup:

Carbohydrates 12.1g

Sugar 6.9g

Protein 11.2 g

Total fat (good monounsaturated fat) 11.8g

Sodium 123.4 mg

Potassium 86mg

Calcium 45.7mg

Iron 0.37mg

Vitamins (vitamin A; B-6; B-12; C; D; D2; D3; K; Riboflavin; Niacin; Thiamin; K)

Calories 69

37. Lettuce and feta salad recipe

Ingredients:

1 cup of chopped lettuce

½ cup of feta cheese

½ cup of canned red beans

1 small onion, peeled

1 small carrot, grated

1 tbsp of olive oil

½ tsp of sea salt

1 tbsp of lemon juice

Preparation:

Chop the onion into nice, thin slices. Salt it and allow it to stand for 5-10 minutes. Meanwhile, mix lettuce with feta cheese and grated carrot.

Wash the beans and cook them for at least 10 minutes, stirring occasionally. Remove from the heath and drain.

Mix the vegetables in a large bowl, add drained beans and top with olive oil and lemon juice.

Nutritional values for one cup:

Carbohydrates 15.9g

Sugar 8.9g

Protein 15.2 g

Total fat (good monounsaturated fat) 10.6g

Sodium 151.2 mg

Potassium 91mg

Calcium 48.5mg

Iron 0.49mg

Vitamins (vitamin A; B-6; B-12; C; D; D2; D3; K; Riboflavin; Niacin; Thiamin; K)

Calories 70

38. Almond salad recipe

Ingredients:

1 large tomato

½ cup of of green peas, canned or boiled

¼ cup of ground almonds

1 tsp of mustard

1 tbsp of olive oil

1 tsp of apple vinegar

salt to taste

1 cup of low fat yogurt

Preparation:

First of all, roughly chop your tomato into a large bowl. Add green peas and mix well. In another bowl, combine low fat yogurt with apple vinegar, olive oil and mustard. Mix well with electric mixer. Add ground almonds and pour over tomato and green peas. Salt to taste.

Nutritional values for one cup:

Carbohydrates 14.9g

Sugar 9.8g

Protein 14.2 g

Total fat (good monounsaturated fat) 11.6g

Sodium 163.8 mg

Potassium 89mg

Calcium 42.5mg

Iron 0.34mg

Vitamins (vitamin A; B-6; B-12; C; D; D2; D3; K; Riboflavin; Niacin; Thiamin; K)

Calories 71

39. Bean and spinach salad recipe

Ingredients:

1 cup of chopped spinach

½ cup of green beans, canned

2 cups of tuna, without oil

1 tsp of lime juice

salt

Preparation:

Combine the beans with chopped spinach and tuna in a bowl. Mix well and season with lime juice and salt to taste. Its a simple recipe but extremely tasty and full of good proteins.

Nutritional values for one cup:

Carbohydrates 24.9g

Sugar 17g

Protein 31.9g

Total fat (good monounsaturated fat) 15.4g

Sodium 125mg

Potassium 73.5mg

Calcium 48.2mg

Iron 0.37mg

Vitamins (vitamin A; B-6; B-12; C; D; D2; D3; K; Riboflavin; Niacin; Thiamin; K)

Calories 108

40. Curry carrot salad recipe

Ingredients:

1 cup of grated fresh carrot

¼ cup of diced onion

¼ cup of sunflower seeds

1 tsp of curry powder

1 tbsp of low fat cream

1 tsp of apple vinegar

½ tsp of sea salt

Preparation:

In a large bowl, combine grated fresh carrot with diced onion and sunflower seeds. Mix well and set aside. Whisk together curry powder, low fat cream and apple vinegar. Pour the curry dressing over salad and add salt. Leave in the refrigerator overnight.

Nutritional values for one cup:

Carbohydrates 14.2g

Sugar 8.9g

Protein 10g

Total fat (good monounsaturated fat) 9.6g

Sodium 122.2 mg

Potassium 81mg

Calcium 45.5mg

Iron 0.37mg

Vitamins (vitamin A; B-6; B-12; C; D; D2; D3; K; Riboflavin; Niacin; Thiamin; K)

Calories 55

41. Chicken with garlic dressing salad recipe

Ingredients:

3 thick chicken breast, without skin

3 cups of water

1 medium tomato

1 large green pepper

1 tsp of ground garlic

1 tsp of apple vinegar

1 tsp of mustard

3 tbsp of Greek yogurt

1 tsp of olive oil

½ tsp of sea salt

Preparation:

Place chicken breast in a deep saucepan. Add water and cook over medium high temperature for about 30 minutes. Set aside and allow it to cool.

In a large bowl, roughly chop tomato and add salt. Finely chop green pepper and mix well. Now you want to cut the chicken meat in small cubes and combine with vegetables.

Use an electric mixer to make a garlic dressing. Mix well ground garlic, apple vinegar, mustard, Greek yogurt and olive oil. Pour this dressing over your salad. Keep in the refrigerator for at least 30 minutes before serving.

Nutritional values for one cup:

Carbohydrates 31g

Sugar 19.1g

Protein 36.6g

Total fat (good monounsaturated fat) 17.5g

Sodium 131.5mg

Potassium 84mg

Calcium 47.4mg

Iron 0.37mg

Vitamins (vitamin A; B-6; B-12; C; D; D2; D3; K; Riboflavin; Niacin; Thiamin; K)

Calories 142

42. Black and white bean salad recipe

Ingredients:

½ cup of canned black beans

½ cup of canned white beans

1 small onion

1 chili pepper

1 tbsp of olive oil

1 tsp of lemon juice

½ tsp of sea salt

Preparation:

Finely chop the onion and chili pepper. Mix with beans in a large bowl and top with olive oil, lemon juice and salt. Serve cold.

Nutritional values for one cup:

Carbohydrates 15.2g

Sugar 5.9g

Protein 14.4 g

Total fat (good monounsaturated fat) 8.6g

Sodium 128 mg

Potassium 83mg

Calcium 41.5mg

Iron 0.33mg

Vitamins (vitamin A; B-6; B-12; C; D; D2; D3; K; Riboflavin; Niacin; Thiamin; K)

Calories 59

43. Greek salad recipe

Ingredients:

2 cups of Greek yogurt

1 cup of finely chopped lettuce

½ cup of finely chopped baby spinach

½ cup of cherry tomatoes

1 tsp of ground dry basil

1 tsp of apple vinegar

1 tbsp of olive oil

½ tsp of sea salt

Preparation:

Use an electric mixer to mix the Greek yogurt with apple vinegar, basil and olive oil. Add some salt to taste. Keep this dressing in the refrigerator for about 30 minutes.

Meanwhile, combine the vegetables in a large bowl and pour the dressing over it.

Nutritional values for one cup:

Carbohydrates 25.8g

Sugar 14.4g

Protein 29.2 g

Total fat (good monounsaturated fat) 18.1g

Sodium 129.3 mg

Potassium 87mg

Calcium 47.3mg

Iron 0.42mg

Vitamins (vitamin A; B-6; B-12; C; D; D2; D3; K; Riboflavin; Niacin; Thiamin; K)

Calories 89

44. Turkey and basil salad recipe

Ingredients:

3 thick slices of turkey breast, without bones

oil for frying

1 small onion

2 tbsp of finely chopped celery

4 tbsp of low fat cream

1 tsp of apple vinegar

¼ tsp of ground chili pepper

½ tsp of salt

Preparation:

Use a frying pan to preheat the oil at 400 degrees. Wash the meat and pat dry using a kitchen paper. Cut it into thin strips and slowly put it into the frying pan. Fry for about 15 minutes, stirring constantly. Remove from the heath and allow it to cool for a while.

Peel and finely chop the onion. In a large bowl, combine the turkey strips, onion and chopped celery. Top with low fat cream, apple vinegar, ground chili pepper and salt. Mix well and serve.

Nutritional values for one cup:

Carbohydrates 28.4g

Sugar 17g

Protein 35.5g

Total fat (good monounsaturated fat) 19.4g

Sodium 155.1mg

Potassium 91mg

Calcium 54.4mg

Iron 0.43mg

Vitamins (vitamin A; B-6; B-12; C; D; D2; D3; K; Riboflavin; Niacin; Thiamin; K)

Calories 148

45. Dried tomato salad recipe

Ingredients:

1 cup of chopped dried tomato

½ cup of lettuce

1 boiled egg

½ cup of corn

1 tbsp of olive oil

1 tsp of lime juice

½ tsp of salt

Preparation:

Peel and cut the egg in a thin slices. In a large bowl, combine it with dried tomato, lettuce and corn. Top with olive oil, lime juice and salt. Mix well.

Nutritional values for one cup:

Carbohydrates 14.1g

Sugar 9.9g

Protein 15.2 g

Total fat (good monounsaturated fat) 11.6g

Sodium 132.2 mg

Potassium 81mg

Calcium 49.1mg

Iron 0.41mg

Vitamins (vitamin A; B-6; B-12; C; D; D2; D3; K; Riboflavin; Niacin; Thiamin; K)

Calories 60

46. Amaranth and mango salad recipe

Ingredients:

1/3 cup of amaranth

1 cup of water

½ cup of chopped mango

1 cup of cherry tomatoes

1 tsp of dried, chopped rosemary

1 tsp of coconut oil

Preparation:

Bring water to a boiling point, in a large saucepan. Reduce heat and add amaranth. Cook for about 20-25 minutes, stirring constantly, until it absorbs all water. Remove from the heat and drain.

Cut cherry tomatoes in half. Combine with mango and amaranth and mix well. Top with chopped rosemary and coconut oil.

Nutritional values for one cup:

Carbohydrates 15.5g

Sugar 10.9g

Protein 15.2 g

Total fat (good monounsaturated fat) 10.6g

Sodium 142.2 mg

Potassium 91mg

Calcium 51.5mg

Iron 0.41mg

Vitamins (vitamin A; B-6; B-12; C; D; D2; D3; K; Riboflavin; Niacin; Thiamin; K)

Calories 71

47. Broccoli and cottage cheese salad recipe

Ingredients:

1 cup of fresh broccoli

1 cup of cottage cheese

1 cup of finely chopped baby spinach

1 cup of low fat yogurt

1 medium potato, cooked

1 tsp of dried rosemary

salt to taste

pepper

Preparation:

Mix the fresh broccoli, cottage cheese, baby spinach and low fat yogurt in a blender for 2-3 minutes. Allow it to cool in the refrigerator for 15-20 minutes.

Meanwhile, cut the potato into thin slices. Finely chop onion and place it over the potato slices. Top with broccoli mixture and season with rosemary, salt and pepper.

Nutritional values for one cup:

Carbohydrates 15.1g

Sugar 8.9g

Protein 14.2 g

Total fat (good monounsaturated fat) 11.6g

Sodium 123.4 mg

Potassium 81mg

Calcium 43.5mg

Iron 0.34mg

Vitamins (vitamin A; B-6; B-12; C; D; D2; D3; K; Riboflavin; Niacin; Thiamin; K)

Calories 67

48. Avocado salad recipe

Ingredients:

1 cup of chopped avocado

1 cup of cottage cheese

1 cup of low fat cream

1 cup of cherry tomatoes

1 tbsp of olive oil

½ tsp of sea salt

Preparation:

Mix the ingredients in a large bowl. Top with olive oil and sea salt. Allow it to cool in the refrigerator for about 30 minutes before serving.

Nutritional values for one cup:

Carbohydrates 10.2g

Sugar 7.9g

Protein 12.2 g

Total fat (good monounsaturated fat) 7.4g

Sodium 123.8 mg

Potassium 85mg

Calcium 45.1mg

Iron 0.33mg

Vitamins (vitamin A; B-6; B-12; C; D; D2; D3; K; Riboflavin; Niacin; Thiamin; K)

Calories 53

OTHER GREAT TITLES BY THIS AUTHOR

www.ingramcontent.com/pod-product-compliance
Lightning Source LLC
Chambersburg PA
CBHW071744080526
44588CB00013B/2147